The Dedalus Press

THE VOICE OF THE HARE

Pádraig J. Daly

The Voice of the Hare

Pádraig J. Daly

The Dedalus Press
24 The Heath, Cypress Downs, Dublin 6W. Ireland

ISBN 1 873790 96 1(paper)
ISBN 1 873790 97 X (bound)

Some of these poems or versions of them first appeared in the following publications: *Cyphers, Poetry Ireland Review, Spirituality, The Merton Journal, New Orleans Review, Spotlight, Other Poetry, Tracks, Voix d'Irlande et du Québec, TESTO, Intercom, Città di Vita, Towards Harmony, Cathcards.*

Dedalus Books are represented and distributed in the U.K. and Europe by *Password*, 23 New Mount St., Manchester M4 4DE and in the U.S.A. and Canada by Dufour Editions Inc., P.O.Box 7, Chester Springs, Pennsylvania 19425

Printed in Ireland by Colour Books Ltd.

The Dedalus Press receives financial assistance from An Chomhairle Ealaíon, The Arts Council, Ireland.

for John F. Deane
and
Jack Harte,
with gratitude for their friendship.

CONTENTS

Three

One

HE

He is somewhere in the garden,
Kicking up the leaves with his feet.

Nothing disturbs him.

He does not care any longer
Whether we eat the fruit or no.

COMPLAINT

I will tell you, Sir, about a woman of yours,
Who suddenly had all her trust removed
And turned to the wall and died.

I remember how she would sing of your love,
Rejoice in your tiniest favour;
The scented jonquils,

The flowering currant bush,
The wet clay
Spoke to her unerringly of benevolence.

I remind you, Sir, of how, brought low,
She cowered like a tinker's dog,
Her hope gone, her skin loose around her bones.

Where were you, Sir, when she called out to you?
And where was the love that height nor depth
Nor any mortal thing can overcome?

Does it please you, Sir, that your people's voice
Is the voice of the hare torn between the hounds?

SORROW

I am eating, drinking, sleeping, dreaming sorrow.
Yesterday I followed a small child to its grave;
Today, an old man.

I watch one I have grown to love,
Beautiful as the wind, languish;
And I flounder in the grief around her.

I sit with husbands in little smoky visiting rooms,
Parsing your reasons;
With broken mothers, with dismayed children.

Your people mutter bitterly against you;
How can I carry them?

MINISTERS

It is we who are kicked for your failures;

When pain lasts across the night,
When people gather helplessly around a bed,
When grief exhausts the heart,
It is we who must bear the anger.

When love fails,
When friends are gone,
When worlds are rubble,
When eyes cannot lift to see the sun,
People ask us to explain; and we are dumb.

When rage against you is a fierce sea
We are the first rocks on the shore.

THE LAST DREAMERS

We began in bright certainty:
Your will was a master plan
Lying open before us.

Sunlight blessed us,
Fields of birds sang for us,
Rainfall was your kindness tangible.

But our dream was flawed;
And we hold it now,
Not in ecstasy but in dogged loyalty,

Waving our tattered flags after the war,
Helping the wounded across the desert.

CHRISTMAS

We listen to the story again:
An exotic visitor
Comes to a countrygirl
In a mountain town
And nine months afterwards
God's wisdom is a footling child.

Shepherds arrive to the place,
Summoned by music;
And scholars from some distant part,
Tracking a light.

But why did not the sun, for awe,
Lose its footing in the sky?
Why did seas not charge across the astonished land?
Why did every horse in every paddock everywhere
Not break into delirious chase?
By what foul means were linnets stilled?

And how can we,
Loving so little,
Fettered by knowledge,
Believe in such excessive love?

MARGARET PORETE

On the fourteenth day, I came to the beguinage;
My rooms were simple and silent.

Outside, the fallen leaves were intensely yellow
As if they held in themselves the secret of light.

From my door I watched the sensuous flow
Of rain along the rooftops;

The pathways were covered afterwards
With limpid waterpools.

I was aware of the Godness of God,
His difference and his nearness.

And, even as my heart was ravished,
I became conscious of enormous evil,
Waiting with book and virtue to undo me.

(Note: Margaret Porete was a Beguine Mystic who was put to death by
the Inquisition in Paris in 1310)

CELIBATE

1.

Funerals, where the desolation of my Winterlife
Answers the desolation around me,
Are easier than weddings,

Where everything speaks of gentleness
And I sit in the warm gathering
With frostbitten heart.

2.

Drained and fully drained
Of all my joy,
Unable any longer

To support their grief,
My flesh cries out
For some enfolding love,

Some ease from the pain
I circle in,
Some place where I can rest,

Who have doled my last drops
On the dry ground
Of your people's sorrow.

EUROPE, 1943

We were thrown on the train like sacks of salted meat:
Women who made small livings as dressmakers,
Women who scrubbed floors with raw hands;
And lived the Torah with earnestness;

Women too whose lives were dedicated to music,
Who scoffed at the sectaries of rabbis,
Who glided through the world, unseeingly,
In shaded limousines;

All of us in one carriage,
With one small bucket between us,
Rattling through sleeping towns,
Wailing silently.

VICTIMS

The proud cities of Europe
Are haunted by their pleading presences.

No railway station is free
From the echoes of their horrible goodbyes;

Each track connects
To their places of slaughter.

Narrow alleys hold houses where they hid,
Fearful of discovery,

Rooms and cupboards where they grew pale
Through hot summers.

We carry the guilt of their deaths
Into our most optimistic convocations.

Even on sunblessed mornings
Their tears curse the air.

FOURTEEN EIGHTEEN

We were the young men of the small towns,
The offspring of labourers' cottages,
The footpeople of the cities;

Saplings becoming trees,
Foals testing their limbs on the turf.

If we walked awkwardly
It was because our boots were heavy;
And there is no graceful way to carry baggage and gun.

Behind us, we left families who loved us
With a staunchness stronger than death;

And you who are All Love
Did your heart too not break in pity for us?

DUN LAOGHAIRE, September 1996

A grey heron in the sky
Flies between silences.

O'Connor's Christ hangs over the harbour,
Above all the partings,
The daily heartbreak,

Above her where she waits for her son's body,
Forlorn
With her agony.

PHILIP

Sandymount, 25-9-1996

1.

Very busy lizzies, forlorn fuchsia,
Last roses of Summer, confident chrysanthemums
Jostle for the last of the sun.

I have come here beside the sea
To be away from your death.
Faith does not console me

Nor reason nor argument
Since you who were
No longer are.

2.

Once we left such an Autumn
For a wet October in Italy:
I recall the sudden descents of darkness,
Your enchantment with lamplight on rainsoaked pines.

Meals in shabby trattorie,
Festive steam of pasta,
You charming your way into kitchens
To learn about sauces from apronned contadine.

I recall your stories of Mumiya and Tiv,
Your boredom with the rain,
Your talk of hurts,
Your mimicry of those who hurt you most.

23

One night when we ended in a bar near the Opera,
You took its depressiveness in hand,
Flattering the pianist into lighter music,
Cajoling an ancient tenor to perform,

Encouraging a Rhinemaiden to sing herself into hoarseness.
People came in from the street,
The owner brought complimentary drinks,
A Finnish girl began to cry.

Your laughter echoed through the evening:
I hear it still,
Echoing
Away from me.

3.

I would see the bright ferryboat
That moves this dusk
Heavily out to sea
As a symbol of your leaving:

But your light
Had no gradual ebb to dark
And spluttered suddenly still.
Now all the laughter is over.

Luxembourg, 8-11-1996

If only the hope in my head
Were the hope in my heart,
I would not be withholding tears,

Now that the stars are out
And I sit with friends
By the window of a restaurant in the Grund,

Eating perfect agnolotti,
Drinking local wine,
Washing everything down with gratis grappa,

Thinking of your excitement
At such a meal, in such a place,
Amid such laughter:

It is as if your ghost has come in
And sits at our table,
Enfleshing your absence.

SARAJEVO

When we came out this morning
We found that they had bombed the park
Which made our childhood magical.

It was a small park where women walked dogs
And old men would gather on warm days,
Gravely discussing wars in faroff cities;

Where children searched under trees for nuts
Or raced through shrubbery jungles,
Tearing the quiet with screams.

There was a pond to the side
With ducks and incontinent geese;
We came there with jamjars to net pike.

There was a space too for football
Where the sun blazed all day,
And corners where light came reluctantly at evening.

I remember it with snow, with ice, in the rain,
        in bright sunshine;
On mornings, full of starlings;
On evenings when we lost count of crows.

Today the birds are gone,
The fowl fed hungry bellies long ago,
A bony dog sniffs nervously in the rubble.

GOOD FRIDAY

He is in the room beside ours
So we keep silent,
Listening to him toss and turn.

Day and night he is ailing
With our ailments.

AFTER CHERNOBYL

for Adi Roche

The children refuse sweets,
Reject toys and picturebooks,
Are sick all day.

They do not understand what is happening to them:
Why they have been brought to this place,
Why their parents do not visit,
Why none of us appears before them without camouflage,
Why we do not touch or comfort them.

They miss the grumbling hens,
The flea-hassled dogs,
The irritable goats,
The wasps humming in the orchards,
The old people chattering before the houses.

Meanwhile in the villages, those who remain
Shake off their clinging homes,
Cleave themselves free of their fields,
Climb lorries to uncertain futures,
Raise cries that pierce to God.

DONEGAL

When that last long Winter had passed
The sun shone again on our peninsula,
Sparkled innocently on the sea.

Bit by bit, the abandoned cabins
Fell into the grass;
Tracks between farms were covered over.

There were fewer people at our gatherings.
The agent divided the land of those who had gone,
Of those who had died.

But the peace over the world is not over us;
The gaunt ones travel the roads of our dreams
In their silent hunger, in their wailing towards ships;

The ghosts of their houses lie weightily on our fields.

BILL

a friend who took his own life

He did not hear the birds sing this morning,
Nor the waters whisper along the dykes.

He did not notice how splendidly the rising sun
Was recreating the sheepcovered hill.

He could not think of the small boy,
The wife, the girls he left sleeping.

In a world of light
He trekked a deep tormented darkness.

In the middle of love
No love could reach him.

On a broad mountain
He walked a dark tunnel,

Untouched by spring, untouched by hope,
From which there was no exiting.

In Hac Lacrimarum Valle

1.

The glowing fuchsia, torn from the hedge,
Begins, immediately, to wither:
As if we needed such reminders
When already the green trees are ravished by creeping gold.

2.

The buildings close around us;
All morning we are waiting for any chink of sun.
Once we dreamt of lands suffused in mercy:
They oppress our waking days.

3.

We gather above small fields to mourn our dead,
Retelling our myth,
Our need stronger than our belief;
Wind blows from the hills; and rains afflict us.

4.

I cannot trust myself to the small lights that shine
    in this darkness.
There is silence all around, a silence so empty
That no bird or whispering insect pierces it,
A silence that cripples all endeavour, a silence to
    break me finally.

PLACE OF DEATH

1.

It tears me apart to leave you,
In all your ravaged loveliness,
In this duplicitous place.

I recoil from the suffocating concern,
The drugs destroying inhibitions and logic,
The carpets and primrose rooms.

I cry against the plausible tongues
Cajoling emaciated bones into frilly nightshifts;
The trivialisers of sorrow, painting gaudy colours on worn faces,
Camouflaging falling tufts with silly bows.

How can we be at home
With people who converse daily with death
And are sane?

2.

Here where people wait to die,
Someone has planted hopeful daffodils;
Tulips cluster boisterously at the doorway.

But the people who walk by us
Have purple daubs on their faces;

And upstairs in her room.
Elizabeth, who vowed to taste death neat,
Asks for morphine, begins to titter.

EXCUSE

Your tiredness was my excuse to leave :
I did not want to be drawn into your desolation,
Look on while your friends kept helpless vigil.

I could no longer watch your spindly limbs
Stir beneath the sheet;
Or offer your pleading eyes encouragement.

I wanted to be away in the sun,
Lost in the uproar of living.

AFTERWARDS

There is somebody else in your room;
But the flowers on the windowledge are our flowers;
And the grief around the bed is our grief for you.

The nurses come and go, offering the balm of efficiency;
Placing a fan, feeding merciful medicines,
Bathing frail limbs, thumping the pillows into softness.

Death must come soon;
And inundation of sorrow
As if this were the first sorrow in all the world.

BLAME

We blame You when life is taken,
Who give life without our asking,
Who hold all life in being :

Every small child, every lamb in the field,
Every daffodil head,
The hailstones falling in flurries on the water.

Our part is to thrill to the pulsebeat of the world,
Exult in the energy of our limbs,
The tenderness of the wind on our faces.

But this ecstasy of earth grounds us;
And when life is taken, we blame You.

THE PRAYER

in memory of Margherita Guidacci

1.

The rain was the heaviest I ever remember in the city:
The bus ran constantly into floods.

At Piazza Monte Sacro
I bought an umbrella and roses.

You were with friends,
Examining a photograph,
Snapped some Summer of your childhood.

You had lingered with the adults
To talk to an old countrywoman coming from the fields,
Your lively face eating the moment full.

Today you are a child again:
Your speech is slurred,
You cannot move without help.

You ask me to pray for your death.

2.

If I were set down again on the street
Where we met after years of letters,

I would know it by the great stones of the Roman wall
That darkened it;

And the rush of steps
Leading to a dilapidated palazzo.

We lunched in a restaurant nearby,
Sitting indoors out of the heat.

I remember a fridge purring beside us,
Arches between the rooms,
Blue murals of Naples.

Our talk coursed down a thousand laneways,
Each of us needing to speak and hear at once.

When we looked into the street again,
Night had fallen.

3.

A friend telephoned with the news of your death;
It was a grey June afternoon.

I put the receiver down
And thought of rain, roses,
A room with high ceilings,

You shrunken as a fledgeling bird;
The prayer you begged for and I could not make.

THE WEARY GOD

He drives his pale flocks
Along the untarred roads
That lead into the hills,

Attentive only
To the noise of their bleating,

The tick of insects,
Ululation of wildfowl;

He has no heart any longer
For the anguish of the streets.

Two

LORICA

Níl tuile sa tsaol ná tránn ach tuile na nGrás

I arise today
To ducks scurrying,
To swans flapping across sun-cosseted waters,
To boats going by the islands,
To terriers barking after crows.

I arise today
To thornblossom skeltering along hedges,
To mock-orange cascading onto high grass,
To blue lakes of speedwell,
To smoke of furzeburning,
To rivers rushing,
To tides spending themselves on the shore,

To the flood that drenches and never ebbs.

ANSWER

He could no longer bear
The aggression of sparrows,
The din of crows in the trees;

And no pity remained in his heart
For the starlings tcheering on the lawn,
Unkempt and hungry after their journey.

He began to berate the God of Birds
Until walking by a mist-swathed sea,
Two swans came towards him,

White and suddenly on the water.

A THOUGHT FROM HILDEGARD

Butterflies are going from flower to flower,
Bees work drivenly among the marigolds,
Blackbirds bathe in a trickle of water.

The pines sway lightly in the Summer breeze,
A lime rustles with enormous gentleness,
Thistledown floats by on the air.

Cars make their way along the valley,
An empty train passes,
An aeroplane drifts patiently across the sky.

I worship Him
Who wears this green and movement as a coat.

CHRISTMAS NIGHT

Cars are scarce on the roadway,
The trees are bare.

A moth crosses my spotlights,
Lingers for a fraction and is gone.

On the radio
They play *In Dolce Iubilo.*

I think of Suso
Dancing through Thuringia,

Calling jubilantly to God,
Enraptured by her.

(Note: Henry Suso is the Rhineland mystic – author of the carol *In Dolce Iubilo* – who through reading the books of Wisdom achieved a deep awareness of the feminine in God.)

GOD

All day long
She has been arranging our welcome:

Scouring down the house,
Sweeping under beds,
Pulling out the old crocheted counterpanes,
Shining glasses and tableware,
Dusting sideboards and pictureframes.

Now she sits in a deep chair
Till we come crunching under the beeches
To the door.

AMSTERDAM BENEDICTUS

Rainfall steadily on water,
On saffron-colour leaves,
On black branches,
On umbrellas held over bicycles,
On buses, cars and juggernauts.

On faces that survived wars and disasters,
On ravaged faces in smoking bars,
On minds torn by the agonies of loss,
On my own mind's dark confusions:
God has visited his people.

God has visited his people,
Soft as figflesh against the windows of cancerwards,
Waking the lone pensioner with clatter,
Falling on estuary mud,
On the sleeping birds,

On the insulted flesh of prostitutes,
On the insulted flesh of cloistered nuns,
On angry people in traffic-jams,
On the sea itself
With its burden of fish.

On all our houses,
On all our dead.
All through the night rain falls,
All through the day;
And falls his mercy.

PRAYER

We gather at the river's edge;
One by one in the darkness
We place our flames on the water.

We watch them drift,
Fragile, flickering,
Out to the unsleeping ocean.

We fear at first that they will sink;
But the water carries them past every hazard
As if it loved them.

DIVINE FOX

The fox comes close to the house
On sunlit mornings of Summer
Before the ladies of the convent finish prayer.

He is secure in his own beauty,
His coat standing out dazzlingly from the grass.

He does not linger;
When he sees us staring, he disappears.

He is there also in Winter
When darkness covers the earth;
And everywhere.

MERTON

The Monk

Coming from chaos
And knowing that he walked close always to chaos,
He sought out this place of discipline
Where he could weep for the pain of animals
And contemplate the fallen sparrow,
Conscious of a God who cares about such things.

Advent

He moves with chilblained hands,
In coarse overalls and woolen cap,
Doggedly following silence;

In the Winter monotony of the woods,
Waiting, learning merely to wait.

The Light of Louisville

London:
Again imagination fails;

Each cardboard-dweller along the Embankment,
Every commuter underground,
The black girls travelling in giddy flocks

All have paths marked out by Love
And each tired face is luminous with unworldly Light.

A THOUGHT FROM TAULER (Sermon 37)

Set the butterflies free,
Let the birds follow, out from their cages;
And the small exuberant pups.

Before you go into your house,
Empty yourself of all thought,
All shapes, all imaginings.

Be at home in spareness and peace;
See how He will come,
Ransacking your rooms,

Tossing everything this way and that
Like one who has lost a treasure;
Opening doors and wardrobes,

Searching under chairs,
Behind cushions,
Emptying drawers onto the floor,

Until He finds you.

LEAVING BRUSSELS

1.

Overwhelmed by chocolate smells,
Sucking a lozenge for a raw throat,
Rain beating down on the airport windows,
I dream of boats on lazy waterways,
Of Memling Madonnas in iridescent fields,
Of Ruusbroec caught into God
Out of the trundling turmoil of the city.

2.

That night rain woke me,
Whispering like an animal along the chutes,
Covering the roof closely like a lover;
I was all joy;
The room was folded in warm wings;
Even in my stillness I was dancing.

A DREAM OF WINGS

1.

He came along the road
In the late evening
When curtains were drawn.

Into every house he put a folded butterfly,
Leaving them to hide
In attics and under stairs

To appear once
Like the grace of certainty,
Flutter beautifully and go.

2.

A butterfly flew across my mind
When all was dark,
Lighting every space it filled.

It stayed seconds and was gone,
But now my darkness is bright
With the dream of its wings.

3.

The butterfly has folded up its wings
And hangs on the ledge,
Absolutely still.

Even the soft breeze through the window
Does not disturb it;

When it wakes
It will carry a silence into the street.

4.

All that time in the darkness
Glorious colour floods its wings;

But uselessly;
Unless the chrysalis falls apart

And releases it to the rapturous air.

BEATITUDE

Footballer

Below in the half-dark
A boy is hitting a ball against a wall.
Now he races out along the field,
Dancing with it, whispering to it,
As if it were a child or a dog,
As if no world but this existed,
As if this were the world that will exist.

Ducks

Beneath them,
Enormous turbulence
As the waters roar over the weir;

But they float calmly overhead,
Rejoicing in the light,
Lazily diving for waterbugs.

Swimmer

Stretching his new body
Along all its length,
He rises through the waters,

Past tangles of seaweed,
Past porpoise and jellyfish,
Past mullet and whale,

Into a light
Where he can float at ease
Forever

JOURNEY'S END

After the tempests
And the lightening at sea,
I am ashore in a sunlit place.

I lift myself to climb the shingle
But my feet give way
And I crawl to the marram on my elbows.

I wait now,
Watching the white perfection of the gulls,
Until He welcomes me.

Three

RELATIVES

Some of them knew little English
But spoke the old tongue
With the ease of skaters ranging over ice,
Of acrobats floating on the empty air.

Their words haunt my words
And I carry the ghosts of their sentences in my head
Like an unsharable secret,
Like a hunted faith,

Like a song I must sing,
Like a lovepoem,
Like a lament.

GRANDFATHER

It was easy for you
(Conscious as I was by then of two languages)
To persuade me you could carry on a conversation
In the dialect of cats.

You would hold the big tabby before you at the fire,
Stand her on her hind legs and question her
About the price of pigs at Dungarvan Fair
Or some secret family matter she had eavesdropped on;
And I saw pattern in her answering miaows.

You had a huge face,
A cluster of curls on your balding head.
I recall walking the Tí' Dóite with you
Searching for mushrooms,
Roasting them salted on hot embers.

You had little interest beyond your fields;
The miracles of the town underwhelmed you;
Drink was *ag ceannach tinnis díbh fhéin*.

You died while I was still a child;
But you were invoked for us forever
As the source of every wisdom.

UNCLE

I never remember him joyful,
His tall figure bending over us,
Talking only of ailment;

Or sitting at the fire in the dark kitchen
While the sun was poured like grace
On the mountain.

There were tales we heard of how powerfully once
    he played the box,
How dexterously he could plait a rope,
How deftly train a dog.

But week after week we never saw joy:
Only silence and pain;
And heavy worry on our father's face.

We grew up under his shadow,
Learning early
How precarious is the human hold on happiness

MINNIE

1.

After all the feuds and squabbles,
The quarrels about trespassing cattle,
The imagined slights,
The carefully hoarded grudges,
The pain (whatever caused it)
That made you build walls of aggression around you,

Like a boat, serenely, on a sea after storm,
When the sun newly lights the waters,
You lie in your hospital bed,
Grateful to the nurses,
Reaching to grasp our hands,
Slipping gently into God.

2.

You put the memories of your oldest brother aside
And the other you had stayed by
Through years of unrelenting depression;

You blocked out the poverty of your childhood,
The mother cherishing secret griefs,
The gentle father favouring your beautiful sister over you.

You constructed a world that should have been;
Where your family shone above others
For the plenty on its table,

The warmth round its hearth,
The brilliance of its children,
The profusion of thrushes in its hedges.

You made isolation a blessing,
Observing every stir the insects made,
Listening to the night-soft muttering of birds,

The hushed tinkle of heatherbells.
You exulted in the hurts you inflicted,
Preserving yourself from the insecurity of affection.

At the end you refused to take food,
Hurrying to die,
Believing that beyond all our tawdry living

Unbearable happiness waited.
There were roads in the past that might have led elsewhere:
A farmer in the Comeraghs you would not be matched with,

A Canadian airman during the war,
Jobs up the country that never lasted.
So I weep,

Overcome by grief and love,
For the life you had
And all the lives that might have been.

3.

You never let us swot a fly,
But made us shoo them gently out of doors;
You cupped your hands around spiders and lifted them
To where they might more blithely string their webs;

You captured wasps in a glass,
Releasing them gently onto flowers;
You taught us to attend to bees in overhanging branches,
To grasshoppers in the windless meadows.

It was no surprise then
That when we gathered for your funeral
A guard of butterflies waited in Seanaphobal chapel;
They fluttered round your coffin,

They landed on forms and windows,
Even on the altarcloth;
They came to offer homage,
You sent them to us as proofs.

4.

Your death was like a healing,
You went so happily into God.
Old friends came for the funeral,

People you had hurt spoke kindly of you
As if whatever caused your rage
Was dead with you;

And we could see in our minds
The little girl who gathered whorts
Till she was black and late for school.

LATERAL THOUGHT

The German family who moved
Into the old farmhouse at Crough

Shocked the parish by shifting their livingroom upstairs
And sleeping near the ground.

In the evening they could be seen in their soft chairs
Surveying all the townland,

Looking beyond the demesne wall
As far as the herd of deer on the upper Bawn.

They could watch the swans ply the river
While we huddled behind hedges.

Looking on, the boy began to know
That the order of the world is not given.

FATHER

I.

Grey dawn through the window
Barely colouring the grimy sky;

Your body like a stranded porpoise
On the hospital bed;

Small discomforts rousing you
From the ease of drugs;

Death tearing you from us
Like a scab from a raw wound;

The uselessness of words,
The uselessness of prayer,

The groans of old men
Waking to the piteous light.

II.

I miss pointing out the brent geese to you,
The spume ravished by sunlight;

Or showing you some new house
In a familiar field;

Or the road they have carved so cleanly
From the mountain;

I miss your delight
In all that changes from yesterday to today.

III.

Of all the things I might remember you for
I fall on something less important:
The bunches of heather from Coolroe;

Perhaps because of how their colour filled the house;
Or that their bells achieved
Such tiny perfection;

But mostly because they were so much ours,
Coming from that patch of mountain
Your people survived on back beyond memory.

Sometimes when you brought in potatoes in a sack
You put a bunch of heather on top
To give them glory.

HOUSEKEEPER

They grew old gradually together:
She was as close to him
As any woman is to any man,

Cooking for him, making beds,
Handing out keys,
Fixing funeral times.

In the evening each one sat alone:
Praying, reading,
Watching news and sport.

They kept separate rooms;
But all night long
She heard his every cough,

Every turn he made in sleep;
Yet she may not rant before his coffin
Or dress in mourning clothes.

YEAR'S ENDING

The crows gather to repossess the woods,
The river follows its silvery way,
The mountains begin to slip into darkness.

Soon only the sky will be real
And the houses pressed like tinsel stars
Onto the rim of the hill.

ASSISI

Francis

There is terror all through the streets,
Sickness ravages us,
Children are taken from their cots,
Mothers die,
Ordinary pimpled youths sweat with fevers.

Storms waste the vineyards,
Rains hammer the corn down,
We cannot lift ourselves out of grief.
Everywhere we move, sounds of mourning afflict our ears;
Marauding armies wait at our gates.

If only he would come,
Moving along some mountain path,
Shabby and small!
Even if we heard some rumour of his journeying here,
We might risk happiness again.

Clare

Beyond the line of rose-coloured shops,
A pathway through olivegroves leads to your house.
People traverse it quietly.

In the refectory a vase of white flowers
Marks your place at table.
We pray, haunted by stories of your beauty

And your sacrifice,
Searching for peace
And deliverance from ourselves.